# Bath Bombs:

47 Magnificent Organic Non-Toxic Bath Bomb Recipes For Stress Relief, Detoxification, Dry Skin And Longevity!

# Contents

## Introduction

Thank you for downloading this book, "**Bath Bombs: 47 Magnificent Organic Non-Toxic Bath Bomb Recipes For Stress Relief, Detoxification, Dry Skin And Longevity!**"

Inside this book you will find information on how make your own organic bath bombs, how to use potpourri and other natural products to create unique products and how to use essential oils to create beautiful scents to suit your mood and personality.

You will also discover the secrets about the health benefits of using essential oils in your bath bombs and you will learn how products you use in your cooking can be utilised to create an amazing bath bomb which you can use yourself or give as a gift to family and friends.

Adding a touch of luxury to your bath time has never been easier and the only thing that will stop you from creating a beautifully scented and therapeutic bath bomb is not reading this book. So what are you waiting for, turn the page and discover the how easy it really is.

Thanks again for downloading this book, I hope you enjoy it!

# Chapter 1 – Equipment

Bath bombs are fun, quick and simple to make, but better still, they require very little equipment. In addition to the ingredients, just five items are needed to make beautifully scented and attractive bombs.

## Mixing bowl

A metal or glass mixing bowl is preferable to one made of plastic as the plastic absorbs the scents from the essential oils needed in the recipes. Although this should be fine when washed, the scents penetrate the material and anything you use the bowl for afterwards will absorb any lingering fragrances. Ideally you should keep the bowl specifically for use in making your bath bombs to avoid any cross contamination of scent on your food.

## Spray bottle

A spray bottle is needed for adding water to the mixture. This may seem an odd way to add the water but even a few drops too many can ruin your bath bomb and make it far too wet and cause the citric acid and baking soda to react, activating the fizzing.

## Gloves

A pair of rubber gloves is advisable when making bath bombs as food colouring stains the skin and can days to fade. If possible try to get hold of surgical gloves as these are very thin but if this is not possible then a normal pair of rubber gloves for washing up will work just as well.

## Sieve

You are aiming to get the mix as smooth as possible so a normal, everyday sieve is all that is required to sift the dry ingredients.

## Bath Bomb Molds

This is the 1 piece of equipment that most people find difficult to get hold of, but it is actually very easy to find. The problem comes when you start to search for molds designed specifically for making bath bombs.

Instead, take a trip to your local craft store or look around on the internet and purchase a 2 piece Christmas bauble. These plastic baubles come apart easily and the bath bombs are simple to remove and are durable so can be reused many times.

They also come in a variety of shapes and sizes. The small ones are particularly useful for making mini bath bombs if you have a little leftover mixture.

If you haven't got any of these then look around your home, there are many things which can be used instead and they do not need to be ball shaped. The molds are only needed while the bomb starts to set so cookie cutters can make a great alternative. Easter egg molds and chocolate molds work well and as a last resort if you can find nothing else, you could cut a tennis ball in half and use that.

## Chapter 2 - Ingredients

### Baking Soda

Sodium Bicarbonate is often packaged as either Baking Soda or Bicarbonate of Soda and is widely used in cooking. Baking soda is an essential ingredient when making your bath bombs as it is the reaction between the baking soda and citric acid that produces bubbles of carbon dioxide, which provide the 'fizz'. It is inexpensive and can be picked up from most supermarkets or corner stores.

### Citric Acid

This is a naturally produced acidic which is found in the juice of most sour fruits. The most commonly associated fruits are lemons and limes but it is a component of all citrus fruits. Most citric acids for sale today are commercially manufactured by fermenting sugar.

### Cream of Tartar

Cream of Tartar is another common ingredient in cooking. It is an acidic that is produced as a by-product of wine making. This is a good alternative to Citric Acid and is regularly sold in supermarkets and stores. If you are adapting recipes, keep in mind that this substitute is of a thicker consistency to citric acid so halve the measure required then replace with cream of tartar.

### Corn Starch

Corn starch is a natural derivative of maize grain and is best known as a thickening agent in cooking. There is much debate surrounding the use of corn starch in bath bombs with many people believing that, while it is good for softening the bath water and feels great on the skin, it can also cause yeast infections. Others believe that the risk of a yeast infection is so minimal it is not worth mentioning.

Personally, I have never had any problems using corn starch but it is a matter of personal choice so in this book I have included 2 recipes without the ingredient and one with.

### Oil

Oil is not a necessity but it is recommended as it adds a moisturising quality to your bath bomb. There are many natural oils available from health food stores, pharmacies or supermarkets, and most are inexpensive. Some popular oils include:

- Almond Oil – Not recommended for anyone with a nut allergy
- Grapeseed Oil
- Rosehip Oil
- Olive Oil
- Sesame Oil

## Food Colouring

If you want to add colour to your bath bombs then food colouring is a perfect and inexpensive way to do it. A few drops can turn a plain bath bomb into something luxurious looking. All you need are a few basic colours to get you started then you can mix them up and create a huge variety of shades and colours.

## Water

A very small amount of water is needed to help bind your bath bombs together.

## Essential Oil

There is a huge variety of fragrance oils available on the market, but if you want to achieve a quality smell, and reap the health benefits, then essential oils are the only thing you should use. A few drops will provide a deep and lasting scent and all the oils have therapeutic benefits. Everything from stress, nausea, depression and many physical ailments can all be helped by inhaling the scent from a few drops of good quality essential oils. As different oils have a variety of benefits I have added a chapter on basic essential oil information, including safety and precautions when using essential oils.

## *Optional Extra's*

### Dried flowers

Adding a sprinkle of dried flowers to your bath bombs adds an additional level of visual luxury, and bathing in water that is dotted with flower buds and petals adds a new level to the pampering experience.

### Dried Herbs

Dried herbs serve the same purpose as using dried flowers, but they do retain a little more of their natural scent than a dried flower does.

### Glitter

While this is not a favourite with everyone, glitter adds sparkle to your bath time and your body. An alternative to glitter is a sparkling body powder. Just a teaspoon in your mix can give you an amazing glow if you are getting ready for a night out.

## Surprise Gifts

To add a surprise to any bath bombs you make as gifts, why not add a little surprise to the centre of the bomb. Theme the gifts to suit the recipient, a little toy, a pair of earrings, anything you like. Your friends and family will love the bath bomb gift on its own and then discover a second gift while they are relaxing in the tub.

## Chapter 3 – Recipes

Here are 3 recipes for a making a basic bath bomb, all very similar but with slight differences to accommodate personal preference. Following the basic recipes are scent recipes blends, some based on health and others based on smell. When you have mastered the basic bath bombs, have fun experimenting with scents, colours and additional ingredients to make your bombs personal to you.

While you are still developing your technique, you may have a few problems with your bath bombs being a little too crumbly, have patience and practice, once you become more experienced you will begin to recognise when more liquid is needed. In general, the smaller the bath bomb, the easier you will find it to compress in the beginning, but even crumbly bath bombs can be used in your baths so nothing will go to waste.

Before starting your recipes, ensure you have your molds and a sieve to hand and put on your gloves.

Use them within 1 month and always keep stored in a dry place. It is best to wrap your bath bombs in a sheet of tissue paper as this will help to keep them free from any moisture that may be in the air.

## *Basic Bath Bomb Recipe 1*

Makes 6 Bath Bombs

### Ingredients:

- 1 cup Citric Acid
- 2 cups Baking Soda (Bicarbonate of Soda)
- 20 – 30 drops Essential Oil(s) of your choice
- 1 tbsp Almond Oil (or other oil of choice)
- 15 - 20 drops food colouring (if using)
- Very small amount of water from spray bottle

### Directions:

1. Mix together your baking soda and citric acid and sieve into a bowl. Give them a gentle stir to make sure they are mixed together well.
2. In a separate bowl, combine your essential oils, almond oil and, if using, your food colouring. Stir well to ensure evenly mixed.
3. This next part must be done quickly to ensure the mixture doesn't fizz. Rapidly stir the oil mixture into the dry mix. It is fine if the mixture becomes a little lumpy. Once it is well mixed in you can loosen the clumps.
4. Lightly spray a little water onto the mix and continue to mix. Add a spray at a time while constantly mixing together. You want to aim for a crumbly mixture which will hold it's shaped when squeezed tightly with your hand.
5. Once you have reached the desired consistency, press it firmly into the molds. If you are using a two part mold, slightly overfill bold halves and then push them tightly together.
6. Leave the molds for 10 minutes the lightly tap the mold to release the mixture. It will hold its shape providing the mixture was not too crumbly.
7. Place the bombs on a little tissue paper and store in a cool, dry place for at least 2 - 3 hours; I leave mine for 24 hours.
8. Your bath bombs are now ready to use.

## *Basic Bath Bomb Recipe 2*
Makes 4 Bath Bombs

### Ingredients:

- 1½ cups Bicarbonate of Soda
- ¼ cup Cream of Tartar
- 10 – 12 drops Essential Oil
- 8 drops Food Colouring
- 1 tsp Almond Oil
- Small Handful of Potpourri or Herbs/Herbal Teabag
- Small Amount of Water

### Directions:

1. Mix together your baking soda and citric acid and sieve into a bowl. Give them a gentle stir to make sure they are mixed together well.
2. Stir in your herbs, potpourri or the contents of an herbal teabag.
3. Follow steps 2 – 8 of above recipe.

## *Basic Bath Bomb Recipe 3*

For this recipe I have adjusted it slightly to make a 2 colour bath bomb. This technique can be applied to any of the basic recipes.

Makes 2 Bath Bombs

### Ingredients:

- 4 oz. Baking Soda
- 2 oz. Corn Starch
- 2 oz. Citric Acid
- 2 oz. Epsom salt
- Small amount of Water
- 10 – 12 drops Essential Oil
- 1¼ tsp Almond Oil
- 5 - 10 drops Food Coloring

### Directions:

1. Mix together your baking soda and citric acid and sieve into a bowl. Give them a gentle stir to make sure they are mixed together well.
2. In a separate bowl, combine your essential oils and almond oil. Stir well to ensure evenly mixed.
3. Rapidly stir the oil mixture into the dry mix.
4. Separate your basic mix into two bowls.
5. In each bowl, quickly mix in 5 drops of food colouring of your choice to create two different colour mixes.
6. Follow steps 4 – 8 of 1st recipes but when packing into molds, alternative your colours so you create a pattern. Alternatively, you can leave one of the mixes with no food colouring so you have a white and coloured bath bomb. Be creative.

## *Essential Oil Blends*

Re-calculate drops to accommodate your recipe

### Mood

1. **Re-Energising:**

   - 8 drops grapefruit
   - 8 drops bergamot
   - 4 drops peppermint

2. **Detoxifying:**

   - 8 drops grapefruit
   - 8 drops lemon
   - 6 drops juniper

3. **Calming:**

   - 5 drops cypress
   - 5 drops lemon
   - 5 drops patchouli
   - 5 drops rose

4. **Relaxing:**

   - 8 drops sandalwood
   - 5 drops neroli
   - 5 drops rose

5. **Romantic:**

   - 8 drops orange
   - 5 drops patchouli
   - 3 drops cinnamon
   - 3 drops ylang ylang

6. **Soothing:**

   - 10 drops lavender
   - 10 drops mandarin

7. **Tranquility:**

   - 6 drops chamomile
   - 4 drops rose
   - 2 drops neroli

### 8. De-stressing

- 3 drops frankincense
- 3 drops geranium
- 9 drops bergamot

### 9. Depression

- 2 drops lemon
- 4 drops frankincense
- 4 drops neroli

### 10. Anxiety

- 2 drops rose
- 2 drops lavender
- 2 drops vetiver
- 4 drops mandarin

### 11. Headache

- 7 drops peppermint
- 5 drops eucalyptus
- 3 drops Myrrh

## Skin Type

### 12. Normal

- 10 drops lavender
- 6 drops geranium
- 4 drops ylang-ylang

### 13. Oily

- 8 drops sandalwood
- 6 drops lemon
- 6 drops lavender

### 14. Dry

- 8 drops sandalwood
- 6 drops geranium
- 6 drops rose

### 15. Sensitive

- 6 drops chamomile
- 4 drops rose

- 2 drops neroli

### 16. Dehydrated

- 10 drops rose
- 8 drops sandalwood
- 2 drops patchouli

### 17. Mature

- 8 drops neroli
- 6 drops frankincense
- 6 drops ylang-ylang

### 18. Acne

- 10 drops lemon
- 10 drops cypress
- 5 drops lavender

### 19. Tired

- 10 drops geranium
- 6 drops rose
- 4 drops cypress

### 20. Broken Capillaries

- 8 drops rose
- 6 drops chamomile
- 6 drops cypress

### 21. Toning

- 3 drops rosewood
- 3 drops Palmarosa
- 6 drops lavender

### 22. Healing

- 2 drops sandalwood
- 4 drops lavender
- 4 drops tea tree

**General Blends**

### 23. Blend 1

- 1 drop jasmine
- 1 drop cinnamon
- 3 drops sweet orange
- 5 drops lime

### 24. Blend 2

- 1 drop neroli
- 2 drops linden blossom
- 5 drops vanilla
- 12 drops patchouli

### 25. Blend 3

- 1 drop jasmine
- 2 drops grapefruit
- 3 drops sandalwood
- 4 drops bergamot

### 26. Blend 4

- 1 drop rose
- 2 drops ylang ylang
- 7 drops bergamot
- 10 drops lime

### 27. Blend 5

- 2 drops ylang ylang
- 2 drops grapefruit
- 2 drops lemon
- 4 drops bergamot

### 28. Blend 6

- 2 drops lavender
- 3 drops cedar
- 5 drops spruce

### 29. Blend 7

- 1 drop ylang ylang
- 4 drops rosewood
- 5 lavender

### 30. Blend 8

- 1 drop peppermint
- 1 drop roman chamomile
- 3 drops lavender
- 5 drops rosemary

### 31. Blend 9

- 3 drops spearmint
- 6 drops bergamot
- 11 drops lemon

### 32. Blend 10

- 1 drop cypress
- 4 drops lavender
- 5 drops bergamot

### 33. Blend 11

- 5 drops lavender
- 5 drops spearmint
- 9 drops sweet orange

### 34. Blend 12

- 1 drop rose
- 2 drops scotch pine
- 2 drops lemon
- 5 drops sandalwood

### 35. Blend 13

- 1 drop jasmine
- 3 drops patchouli
- 6 drops sweet orange

### 36. Blend 14

- 2 drops bergamot
- 4 drops clary sage
- 4 drops ylang ylang

### 37. Blend 15

- 1 drop ylang ylang
- 2 drops vanilla
- 7 drops sweet orange

### 38. Blend 16

- 1 drop cinnamon
- 3 drops sweet orange
- 6 drops juniper

### 39. Blend 17

- 1 drop Neroli
- 9 drops sandalwood

## Men's Blends

### 40. Blend 18

- 2 drops ginger
- 5 drops patchouli
- 5 drops bergamot

### 41. Blend 19

- 2 drops black pepper
- 4 drops lime
- 4 drops sandalwood

### 42. Blend 20

- 2 drops peppermint
- 4 drops lemon
- 4 drops rosemary

## Perfume Blends

### 43. Blend 21 – Summer

- 3 drops rosemary
- 3 drops cedarwood
- 3 drops peppermint
- 5 drops sweet orange

### 44. Blend 22 - Romantic

- 2 drops sweet orange
- 2 drops lavender
- 3 drops patchouli
- 3 drops cedarwood
- 3 drops ylang ylang
- 3 drops bergamot

### 45. Blend 23 - Erotic

- 3 drops lemon essential oil
- 3 drops orange essential oil
- 5 drops sandalwood essential oil
- 5 drops jasmine

### 46. Blend 24 - Woodland

- 2 drops spruce
- 2 drops fir
- 2 drops cedarwood
- 2 drops vetiver
- 3 drops bergamot

### 47. Blend 25 - Flowers

- 3 drops geranium
- 4 drops rosewood
- 4 drops roman chamomile

# Chapter 4 – Essential Oils – Basic Information

Essential oils are the complete essence of a plant and are manufactured using the extraction of the plants useful properties. This is most commonly done using steam or water methods but may also been done using gas extraction. The difference in the results of the extraction is the amount of oil which is able to be obtained and the strength of the oils.

Perfumed or fragranced oils are not essential oils and will be significantly lower in the strength of their scent. Additionally, they contain absolutely no health benefits so it is important to ensure you are using pure essential oils for your recipes. All essential oils will have therapeutic benefits which will have a psychological and/or physiological effect on your body and mind.

Because essential oils are completely natural, unlike pharmaceuticals, they do not build up within the body and yet their effects are often much more beneficial. They are absorbed completely and pass through your body affecting the necessary benefits before passing back out of you.

Despite the fact they are completely natural, they can be extremely potent and should not be used in large amounts. Additionally, there are some instances where they cannot be used which is why I have included this chapter. You must be cautious about who will be using the bath bombs and ensure only the correct oils are used for each person however, when used correctly, essentially oils will help you to create a some beautifully scented, therapeutic bath bombs.

**The following oils should NEVER be used as they have properties which are toxic.**

- **Wintergreen**
- **Wormwood**
- **Pennyroyal**
- **Tansy**
- **Savin**
- **Parsley**

## *Essential Oils & Pregnancy*

The majority of essential oils are safe to use when pregnant, however, there are many which are unsafe during pregnancy and breastfeeding.

Due to the changes in hormones while pregnant, it is possible that oils which you have regularly used will cause adverse reactions so always do a skin test before using.

Skin testing is done by diluting 1 drop of oil in a teaspoon of carrier oil and rubbing onto the forearm. If there has been no skin reaction after 24 hours it is safe to continue using providing it is not an oil listed below.

## Avoid if breastfeeding or pregnant

Mustard
Mugwort
Marjoram
Juniper
Jasmine
Hyssup
Horseradish
Ginger
Fir
Fennel
Clove
Clary Sage
Chamomile
Camphor
Black Pepper
Birch
Basil
Aniseed
Angelica
Wormwood
Wintergreen
Thyme
Thuja
Tarragon
Tansy
Sage
Rosemary
Peppermint
Pennyroyal
Parsley
Oregano
Nutmeg
Myrrh

## *Contraindications of medical problems and essential oils*

Certain illnesses and pharmaceutical medications can cause an adverse reaction when combined with essential oils.

If you have any long term medical conditions or ongoing treatments, seek medical or holistic advice before using:

Nutmeg
Fennel
Dill

**Anyone suffering from high blood pressure should avoid using:**

Thyme
Sage
Rosemary
Hyssop

**Epilepsy sufferers should not use:**

Tarragon
Sage
Rosemary
Hyssop
Birch
Basil

**Anyone suffering with diabetes should not use:**

Angelica

**If you take anti-coagulant drugs avoid:**

Ginger
Clove
Birch

The following oils may be used consistently for a maximum of 2 weeks. You should then take a week to two week break from the use of these oils:

Valerian
Turmeric
Laurel
Juniper
Eucalyptus
Coriander
Cinnamon
Aniseed

## Photo-toxicity & Essential Oils

Exposure to Ultra Violet light can cause skin problems to occur with the use of some oils. This can cause a change to the pigmentation of your skin which varies from a mild to dark change in colour and mild to severe skin burning.

Avoid the use of any product containing the following essential oils for 24 - 48 hours prior to exposure to strong sunlight or a sun bed.

Taget
Rue
Orange
Lime
Lemon
Grapefruit
Cumin
Bergamot
Angelica

## Sensitization & Essential Oils

Sensitization causes skin symptoms which are very similar to those of an allergic reaction. This includes itching, inflammation of the skin, redness and can occasionally cause the skin to become sore to touch.

Sensitization can develop over time with the initial symptoms being a mild irritation of the skin. If the oil continues to be used this will develop into a stronger and more unpleasant reaction.

There are certain oils which are more commonly related to causing sensitization than others so use of the following oils should be restricted to a maximum of 3 to 4 at a time. This should not be a problem with bath bombs providing you are not using the same ones on a daily basis.

- Thyme
- Tagette
- Clove
- Cinnamon
- Cassia
- Bay

# How to Make Your Own Essential Oils

You may want to try to make your own essential oils for use in your bath bombs so the following method is simple and effective. It should be noted though that the quality of the oils will not be equal to the 100% pure oils that you can purchase. Having said that, these oils are being used primarily for their scent and secondary for their therapeutic benefit so will be more than adequate for your bath bombs.

The process outlined below is very basic but it works well and is easy to do in your own home.

1. Gather your plant material and place it into a small crock pot. Fill the pot with distilled or boiled and cooled water and cook on a low setting for 24 hours.
2. Remove the lid and allow the water to cool a little.
3. Remove all plant material from the water. Press or squeeze the plant material over the crock to extract any fluid the plant is still holding then discard the plant.
4. Leave the crock pot to stand, without a lid, for 1 week so the oil and water separate.
5. Collect the oil from the surface of the water and decant into a small, dark container, (preferably a glass essential oil bottle). During this stage it is inevitable that you will collect some water with the oil. Limit the water a much as possible but do not worry about collecting a small amount.
6. Cover the neck of the essential oil container with a piece of cheesecloth or muslin, do not use the container lid yet. The cloth will allow the air to flow while keeping out any unwanted bacteria.
7. Allow container to sit for a further week to give any collected water time to evaporate before removing the cloth and attaching the container lid.

Store your oil in a cool, dark place. Stored correctly the oil will last for up to 12 months.

## Chapter 5 – General Information & Tips

There is no perfect recipe for a bath bomb; they all start out with the same few basic dry ingredients, bicarbonate of soda and citric acid or cream of tartar, this is where the perfect recipe ends. It becomes a case of trial and error with additional ingredients and mastering the technique. A few extra drops of food colouring or oils, the addition of corn starch or potpourri, even adding a sprinkle or two of glitter can throw out the consistency of your mix when it comes to adding the water.

The best advice I can give you is to play with the recipes in this book, practice with them using different oils, different amounts of colourings and essential oils and varying types of additional items. Over time you will begin to recognise when your mixture is at the ideal consistency and whether it is too wet, too dry or too oily and how to counteract it.

- If you find your mixture is very crumbly then it is too dry, try adding another spray or two of water.

- If your mixture is gloopy and sticky then you have too much almond oil or other carrier. If this happens then your bath bombs will not set, whether you leave them a day or a week, they will remain in this gloopy state. You can try mixing a little more of the dry ingredients and sieve them in a small amount at a time to dry it a little but you may have to add an extra drop or two of essential oils too. There is no guarantee this will completely alleviate the problem but if all else fails, you can still use your oily bombs in the bath but they will not provide the fizz in the same way.

- If your mixture is too wet then there is a high chance that the citric acid will activate and start fizzing. In most cases there is little you can do about this but if the fizzing is minor, or not started, you should be able to increase the dry mixture and solve the problem. Remember to mix this in quickly to avoid fizzing.

**Always ensure that bath bomb mixture is pressed firmly into your molds to compact it as much as possible. This ensures there are no air pockets formed within your finished product.**

When combining wet ingredients, mix them together well but do not worry when you notice little pockets of oils forming. This is how it should be and helps to stop the citric acid activating when mixing into the dry ingredients.

**To add an extra special feel to your bath bomb experience, try adding a scoop or two or powdered, full fat milk to your dry mix. While there is no proof this is of benefit to the skin, it certainly feels nourishing and leaves my skin with a silky feeling.**

To give your bath bombs a moisturising element, add a scoop of an organic butter. There are lots of varieties to choose from such as cocoa butter, shea butter, coconut butter or even aloe butter.

**Aloe is great for healing most skin problems from cuts and scrapes to sunburn. Check out your local health store and see if you can find some aloe powder or even aloe tea bags. Adding a teaspoon of aloe powder to your bath bomb mix is an easy and effective way to soothe skin problems.**

Oats are a common ingredient in the manufacture of some bath bombs and are very soothing for people who suffer with eczema. Try adding a small amount of ground oats or oatmeal to the bath bombs to moisturise your skin. (Don't add too many though or you will end up bathing in porridge.

**Never store your bath bombs in cellophane or plastic bags or tubs. These items can produce condensation which will cause your bath bomb to activate before you are ready to use it. Simple coloured tissue paper works really well and looks attractive.**

If you want to present someone with a gift of your bath bombs, package them in a box and cushion them with packing peanuts or polystyrene balls to keep them separated. There is no point going to all the effort of making a beautiful gift only to find they have turned to powder because they have been bashed together.

**Providing you compress the bath bomb mixture well, there is no limit to your creativity when it comes to shapes. Take a trip to the local bargain store and pick up some baking molds in unusual shapes. Why not make a cupcake bath bomb that is layered with different colours. Stick to an average size cupcake mold and get creative.**

## Conclusion

Thank you again for downloading this book!

I hope this book was able to inspire you to create some wonderfully scented, therapeutic and luxurious bath bombs tailored to suit your own personal desires.

The next step is to familiarise yourself with both the scents and therapeutic benefits of some essential oils, purchase the few other key ingredients and spend a short time developing some bath bombs you can be proud of.

Develop unique blends and add a little something extra to your creations so you can make personalised gifts that will impress all of your friends and family, but most of all, have fun making your bath bombs.

Finally, if you enjoyed this book, then I'd like to ask you for a favor, would you be kind enough to leave a review for this book on Amazon? It'd be greatly appreciated!

Thank you and good luck!

## Bonus Section

Thank you for reading this book. I hope you are able to benefit from this.

If you found this book useful, you'll be interested to know more about my other books. I invite you to check them:

<u>Organic Perfume: The Complete Beginners Guide & 50 Best Recipes For Making Heavenly, Non-Toxic Organic DIY Perfumes From Your Home!</u>– Organic perfumes are made up from natural products and contain none of the additional chemicals and synthetic scents that commercial perfumes are made from.

They are manufactured using pure essential oils which not only offer an amazing variety of scents but which also contain therapeutic benefits, so in addition to smelling great, your perfumes could also be treating any ailments or long term health conditions you may have.

In contrast, many commercial perfumes can cause health problems and/or exacerbate some conditions you may already be suffering from, such as allergic reactions, headaches, hormone disruption, increased severity of asthma or eczema conditions, thyroid complications and a suppressed immune system.

These health risks are caused by the chemicals which are included in the perfume recipes and which, because of the secrecy clauses included in the manufacture of commercially branded perfumes, are often undisclosed on the product packaging.

Many of the chemicals included are petro chemicals and are derived from either petroleum or natural gases, and it is around half of these chemicals which are not required to be disclosed. More worrying is that over 300 of these chemicals can be used in perfume manufacture and around 43% of these are untested and have no FDA approval.

The scent of commercial perfumes does tend to last longer than an organic perfume but again, this is due to added fixative chemicals such as Diethyl Phthalates. The possible health costs of regular use of these chemicals in the perfume you wear is extremely high and can include an increased risk of developing cancer, possible birth defects and low sperm count.

An Environment Defence Group conducted a study on the presence of chemicals in 3 new born babies. The findings showed the presence of 137 chemicals. Not all of the chemicals found in the newborns are used in perfumes, however a number of them are.

You may also like:

Soap Making: Made Easy!

Greek Gods and Heroes: The Wrath of Greek Gods, Heroes & Monsters

Dog Training: 31 Amazing Tricks

Candle Making: Candle Making For Beginners

Tidying Up: Declutter Your Life